# QUILTART
## engagement calendar

### 2020

**A COLLECTION OF PRIZEWINNING QUILTS FROM ACROSS THE COUNTRY**

Quilts researched and selected by Klaudeen Hansen

Color photography by Charles R. Lynch

*Best Wishes*
*Klaudeen*

Klaudeen Hansen

**LA PASSACAGLIA**   65" x 74"

**Amy Murphy, Gays Mills, WI**

After viewing many pictures online, Amy decided to try English paper piecing for herself. Choosing and arranging the many colors was a fun part of this project. Amy applied careful cutting of many individual motifs in her fabrics to achieve a special effect. The quilt is hand-pieced, then hand-quilted, one stitch at a time with a "punch and poke" method. Juried into Quilt Expo™, Madison, WI.

Features La Passacaglia Pattern by Willyne Hammerstein, Millefiori Quilts.

Printed in Korea by Four Colour Print Group, Louisville, Kentucky.

## 1857 ALBUM QUILT  89" x 89"
### Lin McQuiston, Rocky River, OH

A reproduction of a quilt made by friends and family of Laura Ackerman in 1857. Gay Bomers made patterns and put them on her quilt shop website as a sew-along. Over 600 people participated, but Lin made her version personal by including silhouettes of her grandchildren. She used hand appliqué and hand embroidery to complete the 64 blocks. Circles, feathers, and tiny pebbles were Lin's choices for machine quilting. Best of Show winner at Lake Farm Park Quilt Show, Kirtland, OH and juried into Quilt Festival, Shipshewana, IN.

Features 1857 Album Quilt Pattern by Gay Bomers, www.sentimentalstitches.net.

# December/January

MONDAY
## 30

TUESDAY
## 31

WEDNESDAY **New Year's Day**
## 1

THURSDAY
## 2

FRIDAY
## 3

SATURDAY
## 4

SUNDAY
## 5

| JANUARY | | | | | | |
|---|---|---|---|---|---|---|
| S | M | T | W | T | F | S |
|  |  |  | 1 | 2 | 3 | 4 |
| 5 | 6 | 7 | 8 | 9 | 10 | 11 |
| 12 | 13 | 14 | 15 | 16 | 17 | 18 |
| 19 | 20 | 21 | 22 | 23 | 24 | 25 |
| 26 | 27 | 28 | 29 | 30 | 31 |  |

### BASKET WEAVE
**Klaudeen Hansen, Sun Prairie, WI**

"There must have been a special kind of magnet tucked inside this Bali pop of fabrics," said Klaudeen. It just jumped into her shopping cart along with the pattern from Cluck Cluck Sew. The quilt was easy to stitch, but keeping the right colors in the right places required concentration. Diagonal setting brought a new element to the design. Machine quilting by Rebecca Smith of Rapid City, SD. Shown at A Mountain Quiltfest, Pigeon Forge, TN and the Prairie Heritage Quilt Show, Sun Prairie, WI.

Features Basket Case Pattern by Allison Harris, cluckclucksew.com.

# January

MONDAY
**6**

TUESDAY
**7**

WEDNESDAY
**8**

THURSDAY
**9**

FRIDAY
**10**

SATURDAY
**11**

SUNDAY
**12**

| | | | JANUARY | | | |
|---|---|---|---|---|---|---|
| S | M | T | W | T | F | S |
| | | | 1 | 2 | 3 | 4 |
| 5 | 6 | 7 | 8 | 9 | 10 | 11 |
| 12 | 13 | 14 | 15 | 16 | 17 | 18 |
| 19 | 20 | 21 | 22 | 23 | 24 | 25 |
| 26 | 27 | 28 | 29 | 30 | 31 | |

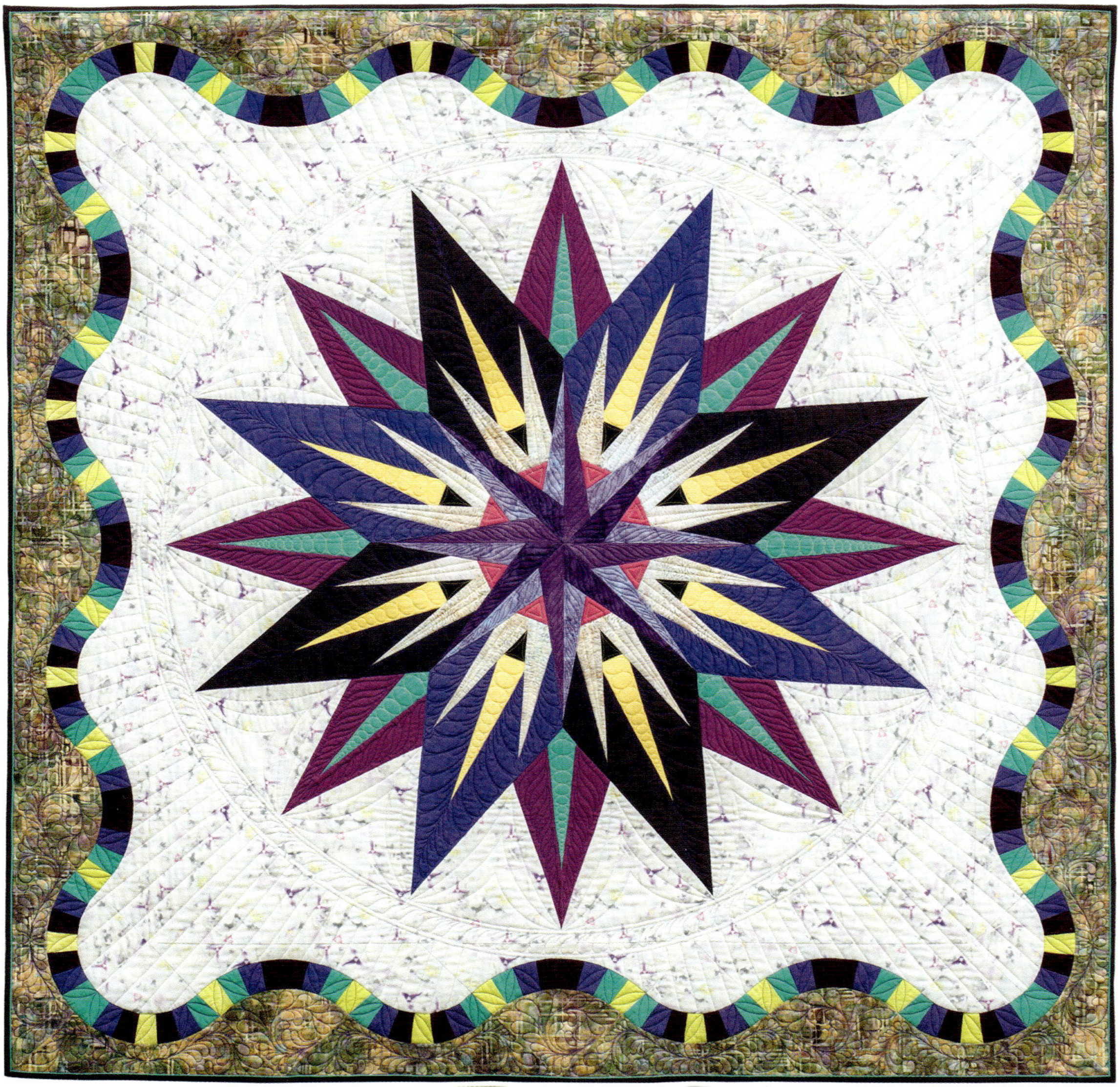

Quiltin' Joy! Helen

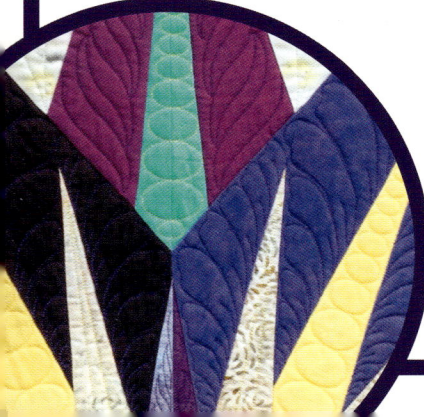

## PRIMROSE COMPASS 60" x 60"

**Helen Smith Stone, Duluth, MN**

Hand-dyed fabric by Joan Skelbeck was Helen's inspiration for making this Judy Niemeyer design. Placing the gradations and adding just the right fabrics was a fun challenge for Helen. The quilt is machine-pieced with a piped binding. Longarm machine quilted by Marlene Hiltner of Foxboro, WI. A ribbon winner at the Minnesota State Quilt Show, St. Cloud, MN and juried into Quilt Expo™, Madison, WI.

Features Vintage Compass Pattern by Judy and Bradley Niemeyer, www.quiltworx.com.

# January

**MONDAY**
## 13

**TUESDAY**
## 14

**WEDNESDAY**
## 15

**THURSDAY**
## 16

**FRIDAY**
## 17

**SATURDAY**
## 18

**SUNDAY**
## 19

| | | | JANUARY | | | |
|---|---|---|---|---|---|---|
| S | M | T | W | T | F | S |
| | | | 1 | 2 | 3 | 4 |
| 5 | 6 | 7 | 8 | 9 | 10 | 11 |
| 12 | 13 | 14 | 15 | 16 | 17 | 18 |
| 19 | 20 | 21 | 22 | 23 | 24 | 25 |
| 26 | 27 | 28 | 29 | 30 | 31 | |

### HEXED  67" x 58"

### Rebecca Smith, Rapid City, SD

Hand-pieced using the English paper piecing method, this quilt was fun for Rebecca to make because of the careful cutting of each hexagon. You can find deer, elephants, fairies, and many other images hiding in these small sections. Machine quilted by Rebecca in matching threads. Juried into Quilt Expo™, Madison, WI and a ribbon winner at the Black Hills Quilt Show, Rapid City, SD.

Features block patterns from *The New Hexagon: 52 Blocks to English Paper Piece* by Katja Marek, © 2014 Martingale & Company.

# January

**20**

**Martin Luther King Jr. Day**

**21**

WEDNESDAY
**22**

THURSDAY
**23**

FRIDAY
**24**

SATURDAY
**25**

SUNDAY
**26**

### JANUARY

| S | M | T | W | T | F | S |
|---|---|---|---|---|---|---|
|   |   |   | 1 | 2 | 3 | 4 |
| 5 | 6 | 7 | 8 | 9 | 10 | 11 |
| 12 | 13 | 14 | 15 | 16 | 17 | 18 |
| 19 | 20 | 21 | 22 | 23 | 24 | 25 |
| 26 | 27 | 28 | 29 | 30 | 31 |   |

## EN PROVENCE  *87" x 87"*
### Gina Nania, Rapid City, SD

Gina chose colors inspired by French lavender fields to piece this Bonnie Hunter mystery quilt. Combining prints featuring bees, flowers, script, and other favorites made this a fun project. Some sections are paper-pieced. Longarm quilted by Rebecca Smith of Rapid City. Displayed at the Black Hills Quilt Show, Rapid City, SD.

*Features En Provence Pattern by Bonnie K. Hunter.*

# January/February

MONDAY
## 27

TUESDAY
## 28

WEDNESDAY
## 29

THURSDAY
## 30

FRIDAY
## 31

SATURDAY
## 1

SUNDAY
## 2

**Groundhog Day**

| FEBRUARY | | | | | | |
|---|---|---|---|---|---|---|
| S | M | T | W | T | F | S |
| | | | | | | 1 |
| 2 | 3 | 4 | 5 | 6 | 7 | 8 |
| 9 | 10 | 11 | 12 | 13 | 14 | 15 |
| 16 | 17 | 18 | 19 | 20 | 21 | 22 |
| 23 | 24 | 25 | 26 | 27 | 28 | 29 |

### THERE'S NO DAY LIKE A SNOW DAY    34" x 46"
**Barbara Riggs, Des Moines, IA**

Creating distance in her original scenes is Barbara's specialty. Raw-edge appliqué is enhanced with tulle for shading and dimension. Yarn was couched on to create the smaller branches, and leaves were textured. Barbara quilted the piece on her home machine. Awarded the first place ribbon at the Des Moines Area Quilter's Guild Show, Des Moines, IA.

# February

**MONDAY**
**3**

**TUESDAY**
**4**

**WEDNESDAY**
**5**

**THURSDAY**
**6**

**FRIDAY**
**7**

**SATURDAY**
**8**

**SUNDAY**
**9**

| FEBRUARY | | | | | | |
|---|---|---|---|---|---|---|
| S | M | T | W | T | F | S |
|  |  |  |  |  |  | 1 |
| 2 | 3 | 4 | 5 | 6 | 7 | 8 |
| 9 | 10 | 11 | 12 | 13 | 14 | 15 |
| 16 | 17 | 18 | 19 | 20 | 21 | 22 |
| 23 | 24 | 25 | 26 | 27 | 28 | 29 |

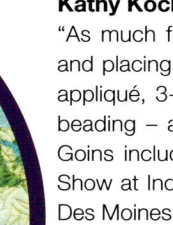

*Love it*
*KK*

## FLORIDA VACATION  92" x 92"
### Kathy Koch, Middlebury, IN

"As much fun as the vacation" describes Kathy's process for selecting and placing the fabrics for this Pamela Curo design. She used raw-edge appliqué, 3-D hand appliqué, and many hand embellishments, including beading – all to remind her of that vacation. Machine quilting by Doris Goins included programmed patterns and free-motion designs. Best in Show at Indiana State Fair, Indianapolis, and juried into AQS QuiltWeek®, Des Moines, IA and Quilt Festival, Shipshewana, IN.

Features 3D Flower Pattern by Rebecca Wat, *Fantastic Fabric Folding: Innovative Quilting Projects,* © 2000 C&T Publishing and Blue Pattern by Pamela Curo, cottontalesdesigns. com.

# February

MONDAY
## 10

TUESDAY
## 11

WEDNESDAY
## 12

THURSDAY
## 13

FRIDAY          **Valentine's Day**
## 14

SATURDAY
## 15

SUNDAY
## 16

FEBRUARY

| S | M | T | W | T | F | S |
|---|---|---|---|---|---|---|
|   |   |   |   |   |   | 1 |
| 2 | 3 | 4 | 5 | 6 | 7 | 8 |
| 9 | 10 | 11 | 12 | 13 | 14 | 15 |
| 16 | 17 | 18 | 19 | 20 | 21 | 22 |
| 23 | 24 | 25 | 26 | 27 | 28 | 29 |

## METRO SCOPE   54"x 72"
### Teresa P. Hecker, Dickinson, ND

The Quick Curve ruler is changing the type of quilts that Teresa has been piecing. She says curves are easier with this tool from Sew Kind of Wonderful. Choosing these bright geometric prints made each curved section a surprise. Each unit was squared up to make assembling the blocks a pleasure. Custom quilted by Teresa on her longarm machine. This quilt's debut appearance was at the Prairie Points Quilt Show, Buffalo, SD, and it was juried into Quilt Expo™, Madison, WI.

Features Metro Scope Pattern from Sew Kind of Wonderful, sewkindofwonderful.com.

# February

**MONDAY**
## 17
**Presidents' Day**

**TUESDAY**
## 18

**WEDNESDAY**
## 19

**THURSDAY**
## 20

**FRIDAY**
## 21

**SATURDAY**
## 22

**SUNDAY**
## 23

### FEBRUARY

| S | M | T | W | T | F | S |
|---|---|---|---|---|---|---|
|   |   |   |   |   |   | 1 |
| 2 | 3 | 4 | 5 | 6 | 7 | 8 |
| 9 | 10 | 11 | 12 | 13 | 14 | 15 |
| 16 | 17 | 18 | 19 | 20 | 21 | 22 |
| 23 | 24 | 25 | 26 | 27 | 28 | 29 |

*Holly Lewis*

## THE DIAMOND BARGELLO   65" x 71"

**Holly Lewis, Cottage Grove, MN**

The way this design flipped from a horizontal image to a vertical image captured Holly's attention. She chose only nine fabrics to use in this Becky Botello design – only nine fabrics, but cut and recut into 3795 pieces! Holly sewed the strata sections first, then cut sections into different widths to create the pattern. Machine quilted by Marlene Hiltner. A ribbon winner at the Washington County Fair, Stillwater, MN.

Original by Becky Botello.

# February/March

MONDAY
## 24

TUESDAY
## 25

WEDNESDAY  **Ash Wednesday**
## 26

THURSDAY
## 27

FRIDAY
## 28

SATURDAY
## 29

SUNDAY
## 1

| MARCH | | | | | | |
|---|---|---|---|---|---|---|
| S | M | T | W | T | F | S |
| 1 | 2 | 3 | 4 | 5 | 6 | 7 |
| 8 | 9 | 10 | 11 | 12 | 13 | 14 |
| 15 | 16 | 17 | 18 | 19 | 20 | 21 |
| 22 | 23 | 24 | 25 | 26 | 27 | 28 |
| 29 | 30 | 31 | | | | |

## INTO THE NORTHWOODS  92" x 92"
### Mary Lou Kerr, Valentine, NE

This pattern appealed to Mary Lou because it represents the Northern Lights. She followed the colors of the pattern, choosing batik fabrics. Bottom Line thread was used for piecing these 2500+ pieces because it is very thin, yet strong. Cotton thread was used for the quilting. The quilt was displayed at the Black Hills Quilt Show in Rapid City, SD and has been featured in many of Mary Lou's trunk shows.

Features Into the Northwoods Pattern by Judy and Bradley Niemeyer, quiltworx.com.

# March

**Daylight Saving Time begins**

### MARCH

| S | M | T | W | T | F | S |
|---|---|---|---|---|---|---|
| 1 | 2 | 3 | 4 | 5 | 6 | 7 |
| 8 | 9 | 10 | 11 | 12 | 13 | 14 |
| 15 | 16 | 17 | 18 | 19 | 20 | 21 |
| 22 | 23 | 24 | 25 | 26 | 27 | 28 |
| 29 | 30 | 31 | | | | |

## ANN'S PINEY ROSES   74" x 74"
### Ann Elizabeth Rindge, Vashon Island, WA
All hand techniques are favorites for Ann Elizabeth. She followed this Cindy Blackberg pattern for the hand piecing sections, then added her own needle-turned hand appliqué and embroidery. Machine quilted by Sharon Stidhane. Juried into AQS QuiltWeek®, Spring Paducah, KY.

Features Piney Rose Pattern by Cindy Blackberg.

# March

TUESDAY

**10**

WEDNESDAY

**11**

THURSDAY

**12**

FRIDAY

**13**

SATURDAY

**14**

SUNDAY

**15**

| | | | MARCH | | | |
|---|---|---|---|---|---|---|
| S | M | T | W | T | F | S |
| 1 | 2 | 3 | 4 | 5 | 6 | 7 |
| 8 | 9 | 10 | 11 | 12 | 13 | 14 |
| 15 | 16 | 17 | 18 | 19 | 20 | 21 |
| 22 | 23 | 24 | 25 | 26 | 27 | 28 |
| 29 | 30 | 31 | | | | |

*"Pieceful Quilting"* *Dorinda*

## RAINBOW KALEIDOSCOPES  71" x 93"
### Dorinda Evans, Madison, MS

Machine paper piecing was used by Dorinda on this pattern from Sassafras Lane. Using all 12 colors of the color wheel, Dorinda planned each block to have the colors flow all around the highly geometric designs. Each hexagon was custom-machine-quilted by Ingrid Whitcher of Pensacola, FL. This entry gathered ribbons at Old Man River Quiltfest, Vicksburg, MS, Gulf States Quilting Association Show, Slidell, LA, and MQX Quilt Festival, Springfield, IL. It was also juried into A Mountain Quiltfest, Pigeon Forge, TN.

Features Arcadia Avenue Pattern by Sassafras Lane Designs.

# March

**16**

TUESDAY      **St. Patrick's Day**
**17**

WEDNESDAY
**18**

THURSDAY
**19**

FRIDAY
**20**

SATURDAY      **National Quilting Day**
**21**

SUNDAY
**22**

| MARCH | | | | | | |
|---|---|---|---|---|---|---|
| S | M | T | W | T | F | S |
| 1 | 2 | 3 | 4 | 5 | 6 | 7 |
| 8 | 9 | 10 | 11 | 12 | 13 | 14 |
| 15 | 16 | 17 | 18 | 19 | 20 | 21 |
| 22 | 23 | 24 | 25 | 26 | 27 | 28 |
| 29 | 30 | 31 | | | | |

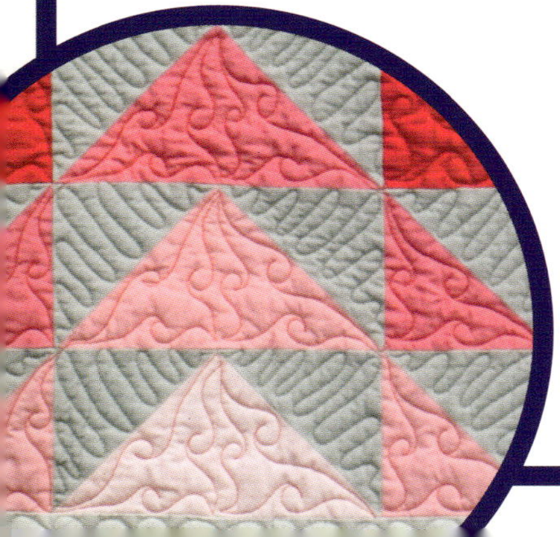

## NEW MERCIES   57" x 72"
### Jackie Clegg, Rapid City, SD

The original title was At Dusk, designed by Erica Jackman for Robert Kaufman fabrics. Jackie spent some enjoyable time shopping for all 30 colors of Kona solids for her quilt. Machine piecing required her to be very organized with all those colors to create the shadow effect she desired. Machine quilted by Marilyn Bates in feathers and pebbles. Displayed at the Black Hills Quilt Show, Rapid City, SD.

Features At Dusk Pattern from Robert Kaufman Fabric Company.

# March

MONDAY

**23**

TUESDAY

**24**

WEDNESDAY

**25**

THURSDAY

**26**

FRIDAY

**27**

SATURDAY

**28**

SUNDAY

**29**

| MARCH | | | | | | |
|---|---|---|---|---|---|---|
| S | M | T | W | T | F | S |
| 1 | 2 | 3 | 4 | 5 | 6 | 7 |
| 8 | 9 | 10 | 11 | 12 | 13 | 14 |
| 15 | 16 | 17 | 18 | 19 | 20 | 21 |
| 22 | 23 | 24 | 25 | 26 | 27 | 28 |
| 29 | 30 | 31 | | | | |

### MY GRANDMOTHER'S GARDEN   92" x 110"
#### Charlotte Schoonover, Rapid City, SD

This Edyta Sitar pattern reminded Charlotte of her grandmother's garden, so she was living on memory lane as she selected the fabrics from her stash. Needle-turned hand appliqué is her favorite technique, and there was an abundance of it in this pattern. She enlarged her quilt by adding an additional column and 20 inches in length. Machine-pieced and quilted by Charlotte on her stationary home machine with feather and circle designs in the borders. A first place winner at the Black Hills Quilt Show, Rapid City, SD.

*Features Reaching Out Original Pattern by Edyta Sitar from Laundry Basket Quilts.*

# March/April

MONDAY
## 30

TUESDAY
## 31

WEDNESDAY
## 1

THURSDAY
## 2

FRIDAY
## 3

SATURDAY
## 4

SUNDAY
## 5

**Palm Sunday**

| APRIL | | | | | | |
|---|---|---|---|---|---|---|
| S | M | T | W | T | F | S |
|   |   |   | 1 | 2 | 3 | 4 |
| 5 | 6 | 7 | 8 | 9 | 10 | 11 |
| 12 | 13 | 14 | 15 | 16 | 17 | 18 |
| 19 | 20 | 21 | 22 | 23 | 24 | 25 |
| 26 | 27 | 28 | 29 | 30 |   |   |

*Happy Quilting Mary Traxler*

## QUILT OF MANY COLORS  86" x 86"
### Mary Traxler, Hammond, IL

Needle-turn appliqué is a passion for Mary, so when she saw this Kim McLean pattern, she knew it would be her next quilt. She spent a year and a half hand stitching with silk thread to complete these blocks. Free-motion machine quilting by Joy Voltenberg. Best of Show winner at MQX Quilt Festival, Springfield, IL and a blue ribbon winner at Quilt Expo™, Madison, WI. Juried into AQS QuiltWeek®, Fall Paducah, KY.

Features Flower Bakset Medallion Pattern by Kim McLean, gloriouscolor.com.

# April

TUESDAY
**7**

WEDNESDAY    **Passover begins**
**8**

THURSDAY
**9**

FRIDAY    **Good Friday**
**10**

SATURDAY
**11**

SUNDAY    **Easter**
**12**

### APRIL

| S | M | T | W | T | F | S |
|---|---|---|---|---|---|---|
|   |   |   | 1 | 2 | 3 | 4 |
| 5 | 6 | 7 | 8 | 9 | 10 | 11 |
| 12 | 13 | 14 | 15 | 16 | 17 | 18 |
| 19 | 20 | 21 | 22 | 23 | 24 | 25 |
| 26 | 27 | 28 | 29 | 30 |   |   |

### BAUBLE 70" x 81"

**Ashley DelaBarre, Bismarck, ND**

This hexagon design by Emily Cier caught Ashley's attention as something different from the usual shapes in traditional designs. She found it a bit challenging to machine piece all the angled seams. The most fun was the machine quilting. Ashley said, "I just started with some straight lines and allowed the designs to flow from my hands." The quilt was awarded first place in the modern category at the Minnesota Quilt Show, Duluth, MN and Best of Show at both the Minot Prairie Festival, Minot, ND and Metro Quilt Expo, Fargo, ND.

Features Bauble Pattern from *Color Continuum: no. 03 emilychromatic: Five Bold and Geometric Quilt Projects* by Emily Cier © 2014 CreateSpace Independent Publishing.

# April

MONDAY
## 13

TUESDAY
## 14

WEDNESDAY
## 15

THURSDAY
## 16
**Last Day of Passover**

FRIDAY
## 17

SATURDAY
## 18

SUNDAY
## 19

| APRIL | | | | | | |
|---|---|---|---|---|---|---|
| S | M | T | W | T | F | S |
| | | | 1 | 2 | 3 | 4 |
| 5 | 6 | 7 | 8 | 9 | 10 | 11 |
| 12 | 13 | 14 | 15 | 16 | 17 | 18 |
| 19 | 20 | 21 | 22 | 23 | 24 | 25 |
| 26 | 27 | 28 | 29 | 30 | | |

## ARROYO GRANDE ALBUM   66" x 60"
### Andi Perejda, Arroyo Grande, CA

A love of handwork led Andi to pursue this album-style quilt. It is primarily hand appliqué and embroidery, embellished with beading, lace, and ultrasuede. Many of the fabrics used were hand-dyed and hand-marbled. Andi personalized several of the blocks, designing cockatiels, rabbits, and more. Straight-line hand quilted by Andi with silk batting. A ribbon winner at both International Quilt Festival, Houston, TX and Pacific International Quilt Festival, Santa Clara, CA.

Features Civil War Bride Pattern by Corliss Searcey, www.threadbear.com.au.

# April

MONDAY
## 20

TUESDAY
## 21

WEDNESDAY
## 22

THURSDAY
## 23

FRIDAY
## 24

SATURDAY
## 25

SUNDAY
## 26

| | | | APRIL | | | |
|---|---|---|---|---|---|---|
| S | M | T | W | T | F | S |
| | | | 1 | 2 | 3 | 4 |
| 5 | 6 | 7 | 8 | 9 | 10 | 11 |
| 12 | 13 | 14 | 15 | 16 | 17 | 18 |
| 19 | 20 | 21 | 22 | 23 | 24 | 25 |
| 26 | 27 | 28 | 29 | 30 | | |

### IT'S RAINING KALEIDOSCOPES   33" x 48"
**Christine Nelson, Tucson, AZ**

Christine owned this special fabric for many years before finally deciding on an appropriate way to incorporate it into a quilt. This original design alternates the strips of ombre fabric with similar colors in her special fabric. The circular kaleidoscopes are hand-appliquéd in place. It was machine quilted in swirls by Arlene Readman, Amberg, WI, and then Christine added a big variety of beads and buttons. Displayed at Quilt Fiesta, Tucson, AZ.

# April/May

**MONDAY**
## 27

**TUESDAY**
## 28

**WEDNESDAY**
## 29

**THURSDAY**
## 30

**FRIDAY**
## 1

**SATURDAY**
## 2

**SUNDAY**
## 3

| | | | MAY | | | |
|---|---|---|---|---|---|---|
| S | M | T | W | T | F | S |
| | | | | | 1 | 2 |
| 3 | 4 | 5 | 6 | 7 | 8 | 9 |
| 10 | 11 | 12 | 13 | 14 | 15 | 16 |
| 17 | 18 | 19 | 20 | 21 | 22 | 23 |
| 24 | 25 | 26 | 27 | 28 | 29 | 30 |
| 31 | | | | | | |

*Kate Philips*

### HERITAGE  93" x 93"
**Kate Philips, Sevierville, TN**

Kate's quilt guild president issued at challenge to all members: a blind color pick to create their next quilt. Kate's blind pick was dark gray. All the other colors were chosen to complement that gray. A ton of pieces kept Kate busy for a while! Machine quilted by Alice Boothe. First place winner at A Mountain Quiltfest, Pigeon Forge, TN and Blue Ridge Mountain Quilt Show, Canton, NC.

*Features Heritage Pattern by Kate Phillips, Sew'n Wild Oaks.*

# May

MONDAY
## 4

TUESDAY **Cinco de Mayo**
## 5

WEDNESDAY
## 6

THURSDAY
## 7

FRIDAY
## 8

SATURDAY
## 9

SUNDAY **Mother's Day**
## 10

| | | | MAY | | | |
|---|---|---|---|---|---|---|
| S | M | T | W | T | F | S |
| | | | | | 1 | 2 |
| 3 | 4 | 5 | 6 | 7 | 8 | 9 |
| 10 | 11 | 12 | 13 | 14 | 15 | 16 |
| 17 | 18 | 19 | 20 | 21 | 22 | 23 |
| 24 | 25 | 26 | 27 | 28 | 29 | 30 |
| 31 | | | | | | |

## OMBRE' MISTRESS  66" X 77"
### Betty Opp and Jan Steele, Rapid City, SD

When Jan Steele came to visit, she asked Betty for a project. This Radiant Glow pattern from Phillips Fiber Art was on Betty's mind, so she shared the idea with Jan. Jan loved the effect of the ombre fabrics and proceeded to piece the top. It was machine-quilted by Marie Brewer with variegated threads in a Diamond Feather design. A People's Choice ribbon winner at the Black Hills Show, Rapid City, SD and displayed at the NE Wyoming Quilt Show in Gillette, WY.

Features Gradient Glow Pattern by Cheryl Phillips, Phillips Fiber Art, phillipsfiberart.com.

# May

**MONDAY**
## 11

**TUESDAY**
## 12

**WEDNESDAY**
## 13

**THURSDAY**
## 14

**FRIDAY**
## 15

**SATURDAY**          **Armed Forces Day**
## 16

**SUNDAY**
## 17

| MAY | | | | | | |
|---|---|---|---|---|---|---|
| S | M | T | W | T | F | S |
|  |  |  |  |  | 1 | 2 |
| 3 | 4 | 5 | 6 | 7 | 8 | 9 |
| 10 | 11 | 12 | 13 | 14 | 15 | 16 |
| 17 | 18 | 19 | 20 | 21 | 22 | 23 |
| 24 | 25 | 26 | 27 | 28 | 29 | 30 |
| 31 |  |  |  |  |  |  |

### DISAPPEARING SPIRAL BARGELLO   91" x 92"
**Barbara Bratt, Columbia City, IN**

Barb made this quilt as a special "thank you" to her husband Tony for all his time restoring her 1971 Pontiac LeMans. She found shopping for just the right colors to create the glowing look a fun challenge. The machine piecing advanced from straight to triangles to a circle before finally becoming a square quilt. Free-motion machine quilting by Barbara in zigzag style on her longarm completed the gift. It was juried into Quilt Festival, Shipshewana, IN and Quilt Expo™, Madison, WI, and was People's Choice winner at the Whitley County Fall Festival, Columbia City, IN.

*Features Disappearing Spiral Bargello Pattern by Koontz's Hand Quilting.*

# May

MONDAY
## 18

TUESDAY
## 19

WEDNESDAY
## 20

THURSDAY
## 21

FRIDAY
## 22

SATURDAY
## 23

SUNDAY
## 24

| | | | MAY | | | |
|---|---|---|---|---|---|---|
| S | M | T | W | T | F | S |
| | | | | | 1 | 2 |
| 3 | 4 | 5 | 6 | 7 | 8 | 9 |
| 10 | 11 | 12 | 13 | 14 | 15 | 16 |
| 17 | 18 | 19 | 20 | 21 | 22 | 23 |
| 24 | 25 | 26 | 27 | 28 | 29 | 30 |
| 31 | | | | | | |

### PRAIRIE BLOSSOMS   86" x 95"
**Prairie Points Quilt Guild Members, Buffalo, SD**

Laura Johnson designed this appliqué quilt for each participant to add her own embellishment. It includes yarn, rickrack, netting, and buttons. Block makers are Kay Baier, Shirley Clarkson, Janet DeBow, Pennee Clanton, Ruth Haas, Laura Johnson, Kay Ovitz, Linda Paulson, Ann Parfrey, Karen Stevenson, and Rita Thompson. Machine quilted by Brenda Tanovy. Unveiled at the Prairie Points Memorial Day Quilt Show, Buffalo, SD and displayed at the Central States Fair, Rapid City, SD.

# May

**Memorial Day**

TUESDAY

**26**

WEDNESDAY

**27**

THURSDAY

**28**

FRIDAY

**29**

SATURDAY

**30**

SUNDAY

**31**

| | | | MAY | | | |
|---|---|---|---|---|---|---|
| S | M | T | W | T | F | S |
| | | | | | 1 | 2 |
| 3 | 4 | 5 | 6 | 7 | 8 | 9 |
| 10 | 11 | 12 | 13 | 14 | 15 | 16 |
| 17 | 18 | 19 | 20 | 21 | 22 | 23 |
| 24 | 25 | 26 | 27 | 28 | 29 | 30 |
| 31 | | | | | | |

## HAPPY AS A CLAM  66" x 68"
### Monique Baczewski, Marana, AZ

Attending a class by the designer, Karolyn Jensen, gave Monique the special skills for paper piecing and applying piping needed to make this quilt. Fabrics were primarily by Moda. Machine quilted by Becky Coykendall of Creative Lines Quilting. A ribbon winner at Quilt Fiesta, Tucson, AZ, the quilt is a big winner with Monique's mother; she loves having it hang on the wall in her piano room.

Features Pickled Clams with Floating Edge Finish Pattern by Karolyn "Nubin" Jensen, NubinQuilts.com.

# June

**MONDAY**

## 1

**TUESDAY**

## 2

**WEDNESDAY**

## 3

**THURSDAY**

## 4

**FRIDAY**

## 5

**SATURDAY**

## 6

**SUNDAY**

## 7

| JUNE | | | | | | |
|---|---|---|---|---|---|---|
| S | M | T | W | T | F | S |
| | 1 | 2 | 3 | 4 | 5 | 6 |
| 7 | 8 | 9 | 10 | 11 | 12 | 13 |
| 14 | 15 | 16 | 17 | 18 | 19 | 20 |
| 21 | 22 | 23 | 24 | 25 | 26 | 27 |
| 28 | 29 | 30 | | | | |

*Nancy B Blake*

## BIRDS AND THE BEE 75" x 86"

### Nancy B. Blake, Madison, WI

Japanese bird fabric inspired Nancy to apply her original concept to the traditional Wedding Ring pattern. She loves curved piecing by machine and finds it well-suited to modern interpretations. The quilt was machine quilted by Norma Riehm, following many of the fabric motifs. Prairie Heritage Quilt Show in Sun Prairie, WI and the Minnesota State show in St. Cloud both designated it a blue ribbon winner. Another ribbon was added to Nancy's collection at Quilt Expo™, Madison, WI.

# June

**8**

TUESDAY
**9**

WEDNESDAY
**10**

THURSDAY
**11**

FRIDAY
**12**

SATURDAY
**13**

SUNDAY       **Flag Day**
**14**

JUNE

| S | M | T | W | T | F | S |
|---|---|---|---|---|---|---|
|   | 1 | 2 | 3 | 4 | 5 | 6 |
| 7 | 8 | 9 | 10 | 11 | 12 | 13 |
| 14 | 15 | 16 | 17 | 18 | 19 | 20 |
| 21 | 22 | 23 | 24 | 25 | 26 | 27 |
| 28 | 29 | 30 |   |   |   |   |

*Carolyn Clark Mack*

**NORTH & SOUTH** 70" x 93"

**Carolyn Mack, Geneva, IL**

Color choice and arrangement was an enjoyable but time-consuming process for Carolyn. The pattern was made by Nichole Ramirez for Kaufman Fabrics. Machine-pieced, then quilted by Carolyn on her Innova longarm. She used ruler work complemented with hand-guided feathers. A ribbon winner at Prairie Star Guild Show, Grand Rivers, KY and juried into Quilt Festival, Shipshewana, IN.

Features North and South Pattern by Nichole Ramirez, robertkaufman.com.

# June

**MONDAY**
## 15

**TUESDAY**
## 16

**WEDNESDAY**
## 17

**THURSDAY**
## 18

**FRIDAY**
## 19

**SATURDAY**
## 20

**SUNDAY**
## 21

**Father's Day**

JUNE

| S | M | T | W | T | F | S |
|---|---|---|---|---|---|---|
|   | 1 | 2 | 3 | 4 | 5 | 6 |
| 7 | 8 | 9 | 10 | 11 | 12 | 13 |
| 14 | 15 | 16 | 17 | 18 | 19 | 20 |
| 21 | 22 | 23 | 24 | 25 | 26 | 27 |
| 28 | 29 | 30 |   |   |   |   |

### POP-UP POSIES  57" x 57"
### Erin Russek, Louisville, CO

A serious enjoyment of garden flowers, along with the absence of a green thumb, led Erin to design her own floral quilt. Flowers, leaves, and setting curves are all hand appliquéd by Erin. Machine quilted by Karen McTavish. The quilt was juried into AQS QuiltWeek®, Spring Paducah, KY and Road to California, Ontario, CA.

# June

MONDAY
## 22

TUESDAY
## 23

WEDNESDAY
## 24

THURSDAY
## 25

FRIDAY
## 26

SATURDAY
## 27

SUNDAY
## 28

JUNE

| S | M | T | W | T | F | S |
|---|---|---|---|---|---|---|
|   |   | 1 | 2 | 3 | 4 | 5 | 6 |
| 7 | 8 | 9 | 10 | 11 | 12 | 13 |
| 14 | 15 | 16 | 17 | 18 | 19 | 20 |
| 21 | 22 | 23 | 24 | 25 | 26 | 27 |
| 28 | 29 | 30 |   |   |   |   |

### GETTING TO KNOW HUE   94" x 99"
### Debra Yeik, Veteran, WY

This block-of-the-month design by Nancy Rink was started by Debra in February 2017, and the top was finished a year later. Debra enjoyed both the piecing and appliqué sections. She had been a longarm quilter for only a year and did both freehand designs and ruler work on her quilt, which was a blue ribbon winner at the Black Hills Quilt Show, Rapid City, SD.

Features Getting To Know Hue Pattern By Nancy Rink, Nancy Rink Designs.

# June/July

MONDAY
## 29

TUESDAY
## 30

WEDNESDAY
## 1

THURSDAY
## 2

FRIDAY
## 3

SATURDAY          **Independence Day**
## 4

SUNDAY
## 5

| JULY | | | | | | |
|---|---|---|---|---|---|---|
| S | M | T | W | T | F | S |
| | | | 1 | 2 | 3 | 4 |
| 5 | 6 | 7 | 8 | 9 | 10 | 11 |
| 12 | 13 | 14 | 15 | 16 | 17 | 18 |
| 19 | 20 | 21 | 22 | 23 | 24 | 25 |
| 26 | 27 | 28 | 29 | 30 | 31 | |

### MY GARDEN  62" x 62"
**Nancy Devendorf Ware, Campbellsport, WI**

Embroidery is a favorite pastime for Nancy, so this Round the Garden pattern by Wendy Williams caught her attention. She used hand appliqué with felted wool on cotton background fabric. Embroidered with pearl cotton thread. A winner at Winter Quilt Show, West Bend, WI and juried into AQS QuiltWeek®, Spring Paducah, KY and Quilt Expo™, Madison, WI.

*Nancy Ware*

Original pattern by Wendy Williams from flyingfishkits.com.au.

# July

MONDAY
## 6


TUESDAY
## 7


WEDNESDAY
## 8


THURSDAY
## 9


FRIDAY
## 10


SATURDAY
## 11


SUNDAY
## 12

JULY

| S | M | T | W | T | F | S |
|---|---|---|---|---|---|---|
|   |   |   | 1 | 2 | 3 | 4 |
| 5 | 6 | 7 | 8 | 9 | 10 | 11 |
| 12 | 13 | 14 | 15 | 16 | 17 | 18 |
| 19 | 20 | 21 | 22 | 23 | 24 | 25 |
| 26 | 27 | 28 | 29 | 30 | 31 |   |

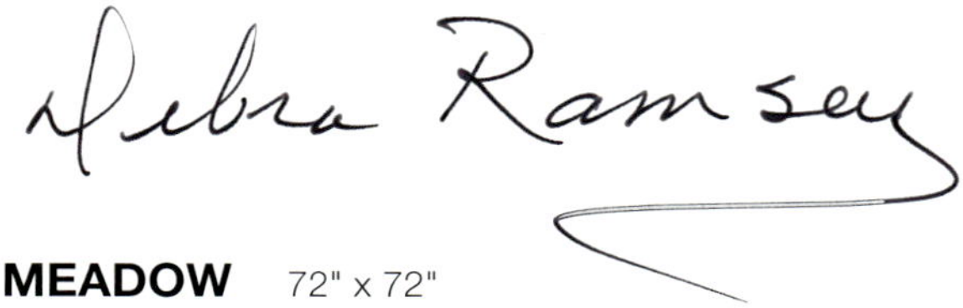

*Debra Ramsey*

## MEADOW   72" x 72"

### Debra Ramsey, Lexington, OH

This McKenna Ryan pattern was fun for Debra; she chose all the fabrics from her stash to achieve the look she had in her mind. The tree block was the most difficult, but worth the extra effort to include the tiny woodland animals. Raw-edge machine appliqué is embellished with embroidery using variegated pearl cotton. Quilted by Debra on her Elna domestic machine with a variety of background fills. Juried into AQS QuiltWeek®, Daytona, FL.

Features Petals of My Heart II Pattern by McKenna Ryan, McKenna Ryan Designs.

# July

MONDAY
## 13

TUESDAY
## 14

WEDNESDAY
## 15

THURSDAY
## 16

FRIDAY
## 17

SATURDAY
## 18

SUNDAY
## 19

JULY

| S | M | T | W | T | F | S |
|---|---|---|---|---|---|---|
|   |   |   | 1 | 2 | 3 | 4 |
| 5 | 6 | 7 | 8 | 9 | 10 | 11 |
| 12 | 13 | 14 | 15 | 16 | 17 | 18 |
| 19 | 20 | 21 | 22 | 23 | 24 | 25 |
| 26 | 27 | 28 | 29 | 30 | 31 |   |

### MY MONARCH   98" x 102"
### Jennifer P. Golden, Sheridan, WY

Creating mirror images was a challenge, but fun for Jennifer. Choosing fabrics was a process that went on until quilt was complete, requiring many trips to The Quilter's Fix quilt shop to find the perfect fall fabrics. Free-motion machine quilted by Tae Yamaki of Fort Collins, CO. A ribbon winner at Black Hills Quilt Show, Rapid City, SD, Wyoming State Guild Show, Riverton, WY, and NE Wyoming Quilt Show, Gillette, WY.

*Features My Butterfly Pattern by Tula Pink, tulapink.com.*

# Order now for another year of spectacular quilts

# QUILTART™ 2021
## by Klaudeen Hansen

## QUILTART™
## 2021 ENGAGEMENT CALENDAR
## AVAILABLE APRIL 15, 2020

Spend 2021 with 54 gorgeous quilts in hand as you jot your reminders, appointments, and to-do lists on the spacious, dated pages of the QuiltArt 2021 Engagement Calendar. Each week, enjoy another stunning quilt chosen by Klaudeen Hansen as you turn the page. A sturdy spiral binding allows the pages to lie flat for easy writing. Great for gifting and quilt journaling!
#11628, 7" x 9", 128 pages . . . . . . . . . $15.95

## To Place An Order
8:00 a.m. through 4:00 p.m. CST M–F

# 1-800-626-5420

- - - - - - - - - - **Detach and Return** - - - - - - - - - -

#11628    QUILT ART™ 2020 ENGAGEMENT CALENDAR @ $15.95
#15095    QUILT ART™ 2021 ENGAGEMENT CALENDAR @ $15.95

For more information on becoming a member of AQS, check here ☐ **#2323**

*Postage & Handling   _____

KY residents add 6% sales tax   _____

TOTAL ENCLOSED   _____

## Method of Payment
Make checks payable to American Quilter's Society.

I have enclosed a check for $ _____ Ck# _____

Charge my:

☐ MasterCard   ☐ VISA   ☐ DISCOVER NOVUS   ☐ AMERICAN EXPRESS   Exp. _____

Card # ☐☐☐☐ ☐☐☐☐ ☐☐☐☐ ☐☐☐☐ ☐☐☐☐

Signature _____

Name _____

Address _____

City _____ State _____ Zip _____

Country _____

American Quilter's Society
PO Box 3290 • Paducah, KY 42002-3290
Phone: 270-898-7903 • FAX: 270-898-1173
www.shopAQS.com

# American Quilter's Society

## JOIN FOR JUST $25

Receive **6** issues of ***AQ magazine***
and all the benefits of AQS

**Join now at - americanquilter.com/AQS**

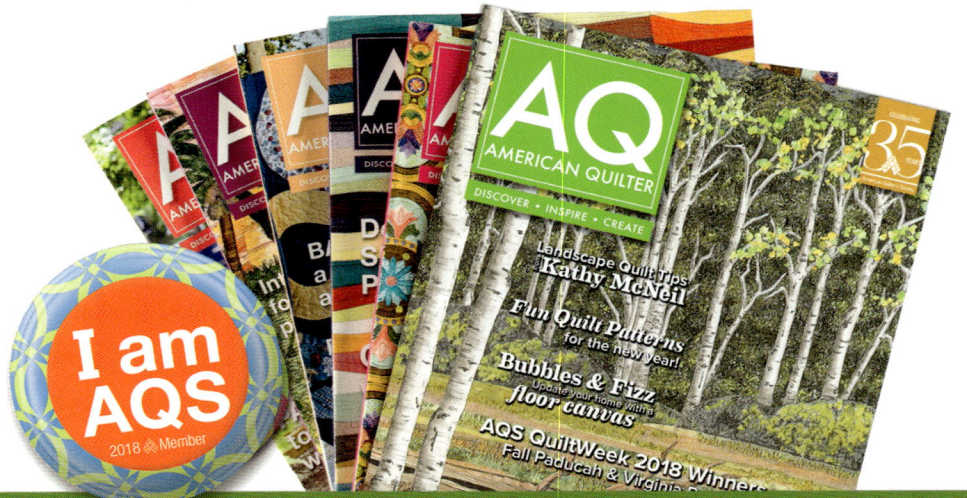

## I want to be part of AQS!

### Become a member and receive these exciting benefits!

- **6** issues of ***AQ*** magazine
- **20% off** at ShopAQS.com
- **20% off** online classes at iquilt.com
- **20% off** AQS QuiltWeek booth
- **Early access and discounts** on registration for AQS QuiltWeek
- **Hertz car rental discount**
- **The Perkspot national discount program**
- **Members Only –** free patterns, articles & web exclusives

# July

**MONDAY**
## 20

**TUESDAY**
## 21

**WEDNESDAY**
## 22

**THURSDAY**
## 23

**FRIDAY**
## 24

**SATURDAY**
## 25

**SUNDAY**
## 26

### JULY

| S | M | T | W | T | F | S |
|---|---|---|---|---|---|---|
|   |   |   | 1 | 2 | 3 | 4 |
| 5 | 6 | 7 | 8 | 9 | 10 | 11 |
| 12 | 13 | 14 | 15 | 16 | 17 | 18 |
| 19 | 20 | 21 | 22 | 23 | 24 | 25 |
| 26 | 27 | 28 | 29 | 30 | 31 |   |

## MY NEW YORK BEAUTY    65" x 77"
### Kathryn E. Wald, Tucson, AZ

There are 185 different cotton fabrics in this pieced quilt. Kathryn started with fabrics from her stash and then had fun shopping for some additional pieces. She used a Karen Stone pattern for the paper piecing. The border was added from a different pattern, also by Karen Stone. The quilt was machine-quilted by Linda Powell of Avondale, AZ on her computer-guided longarm. Displayed at Quilt Fiesta, Tucson, AZ.

Features Variations Pattern by Karen K. Stone, from *Karen K. Stone MORE Quilts,* © 2012 The Electric Quilt Company

# July/August

**MONDAY**
## 27

**TUESDAY**
## 28

**WEDNESDAY**
## 29

**THURSDAY**
## 30

**FRIDAY**
## 31

**SATURDAY**
## 1

**SUNDAY**
## 2

| AUGUST | | | | | | |
|---|---|---|---|---|---|---|
| S | M | T | W | T | F | S |
| | | | | | | 1 |
| 2 | 3 | 4 | 5 | 6 | 7 | 8 |
| 9 | 10 | 11 | 12 | 13 | 14 | 15 |
| 16 | 17 | 18 | 19 | 20 | 21 | 22 |
| 23 | 24 | 25 | 26 | 27 | 28 | 29 |
| 30 | 31 | | | | | |

## GARDEN PARTY   66" x 87"
### Kathy Miller, Rapid City, SD

It was "sew" much fun to create a garden of flowers and butterflies from this rainbow of fabrics. No two flowers or butterflies are alike in this pattern by Laura Heine. Machine appliquéd and machine pieced by Kathy. Marie Brewer continued to make the flowers unique by machine quilting a different pattern on each petal. The quilt was awarded a blue ribbon and a judge's choice ribbon at the Black Hills Quilt Show in Rapid City, SD.

*Features Garden Party Pattern by Laura Heine.*

# August

**MONDAY**

**3**

**TUESDAY**

**4**

**WEDNESDAY**

**5**

**THURSDAY**

**6**

**FRIDAY**

**7**

**SATURDAY**

**8**

**SUNDAY**

**9**

| AUGUST | | | | | | |
|---|---|---|---|---|---|---|
| S | M | T | W | T | F | S |
|  |  |  |  |  |  | 1 |
| 2 | 3 | 4 | 5 | 6 | 7 | 8 |
| 9 | 10 | 11 | 12 | 13 | 14 | 15 |
| 16 | 17 | 18 | 19 | 20 | 21 | 22 |
| 23 | 24 | 25 | 26 | 27 | 28 | 29 |
| 30 | 31 |  |  |  |  |  |

## MOUNTAIN ROSE  96"x 96"

### Cathy Bullman Stines, Marshall, NC

Judy Niemeyer's patterns are addicting, according to Cathy. She has made several of Judy's designs and says it is very gratifying to see the tons of pieces and colors come together when the piecing is finished. This one features all batik fabrics and was machine quilted by Valerie Wagoner. It was shown at A Mountain Quiltfest, Pigeon Forge, TN.

Features Vintage Rose Pattern by Judy and Bradley Niemeyer, www.quiltworx.com

# August

MONDAY
## 10

TUESDAY
## 11

WEDNESDAY
## 12

THURSDAY
## 13

FRIDAY
## 14

SATURDAY
## 15

SUNDAY
## 16

| AUGUST | | | | | | |
|---|---|---|---|---|---|---|
| S | M | T | W | T | F | S |
|  |  |  |  |  |  | 1 |
| 2 | 3 | 4 | 5 | 6 | 7 | 8 |
| 9 | 10 | 11 | 12 | 13 | 14 | 15 |
| 16 | 17 | 18 | 19 | 20 | 21 | 22 |
| 23 | 24 | 25 | 26 | 27 | 28 | 29 |
| 30 | 31 |  |  |  |  |  |

### MERRIMENT  72" x 80"
### Marj Luchtenburg, Waukee, IA

Choosing unusual and fun fabrics from her collection was an experiment for Marj when making this pattern by Wendy Williams. The most fun part was watching the large flowers and leaves make a sweeping presence around the Nine-Patches. Marj did her own machine quilting. A ribbon winner in both the Des Moines Area Quilt Guild Show, Des Moines, IA and the Garden Quilt Show in Ames, IA.

Features Growing Up Pattern by Wendy Williams, ©2013 *Quiltmania* magazine.

# August

MONDAY
## 17

TUESDAY
## 18

WEDNESDAY
## 19

THURSDAY
## 20

FRIDAY
## 21

SATURDAY
## 22

SUNDAY
## 23

AUGUST

| S | M | T | W | T | F | S |
|---|---|---|---|---|---|---|
|   |   |   |   |   |   | 1 |
| 2 | 3 | 4 | 5 | 6 | 7 | 8 |
| 9 | 10 | 11 | 12 | 13 | 14 | 15 |
| 16 | 17 | 18 | 19 | 20 | 21 | 22 |
| 23 | 24 | 25 | 26 | 27 | 28 | 29 |
| 30 | 31 |   |   |   |   |   |

## LET'S PLAY WITH FRIENDS   60 " x 71"
### Candy Hargrove, Kansas City, MO

A collection of fabrics from Moda, designed by Carey Yoder, was the inspiration for Candy to make a lot of traditional blocks. Machine piecing and hand appliqué techniques were used to create various block sizes, and then she put the puzzle together in her own original setting. Custom machine quilting by Diane Juranich. Awarded a blue ribbon at the Kansas City Regional Quilt Festival, Kansas City, MO and juried into AQS Spring QuiltWeek®, Paducah, KY.

# August

**24**

TUESDAY
**25**

WEDNESDAY
**26**

THURSDAY
**27**

FRIDAY
**28**

SATURDAY
**29**

SUNDAY
**30**

| AUGUST | | | | | | |
|---|---|---|---|---|---|---|
| S | M | T | W | T | F | S |
|  |  |  |  |  |  | 1 |
| 2 | 3 | 4 | 5 | 6 | 7 | 8 |
| 9 | 10 | 11 | 12 | 13 | 14 | 15 |
| 16 | 17 | 18 | 19 | 20 | 21 | 22 |
| 23 | 24 | 25 | 26 | 27 | 28 | 29 |
| 30 | 31 |  |  |  |  |  |

### IN HARMONY   47" x 47"
### Naida Koraly, Cape Carteret, NC

Creating original designs is the highlight of Naida's quilting life. This one represents her joy in living near the ocean and her husband's love of adventure in the mountains. Pulling fabrics from only her stash to use was totally fun... until she realized the mess she has made in her studio! This piece is primarily raw-edge appliqué fused to muslin and quilted on Naida's Sweet Sixteen Handi Quilter machine. It was juried into AQS QuiltWeek®, Fall Paducah, KY and Grand Rapids, MI. The Crystal Coast Quilt Show in Morehead, NC awarded Naida a ribbon for this innovative art piece.

# August/September

MONDAY
## 31

TUESDAY
## 1

WEDNESDAY
## 2

THURSDAY
## 3

FRIDAY
## 4

SATURDAY
## 5

SUNDAY
## 6

### SEPTEMBER

| S | M | T | W | T | F | S |
|---|---|---|---|---|---|---|
|   |   | 1 | 2 | 3 | 4 | 5 |
| 6 | 7 | 8 | 9 | 10 | 11 | 12 |
| 13 | 14 | 15 | 16 | 17 | 18 | 19 |
| 20 | 21 | 22 | 23 | 24 | 25 | 26 |
| 27 | 28 | 29 | 30 |   |   |   |

## ART & CRAFTS SAMPLER QUILT   61" x 73"
### Judy Struck, Schaumburg, IL

Michele Hill designed this William Morris-style quilt and the fabrics that were used by Judy to appliqué the blocks. Judy used blanket stitching by hand around each piece. She started the project as a block-of-the-month, but spent much more than a month on each block! Jody York-Caraballo did the machine quilting. The quilt was juried into Quilt Expo™, Madison, WI.

Features Arts & Crafts Sampler Quilt Pattern by Michele Hill.

# September

**MONDAY**
## 7
**Labor Day**

**TUESDAY**
## 8

**WEDNESDAY**
## 9

**THURSDAY**
## 10

**FRIDAY**
## 11

**SATURDAY**
## 12

**SUNDAY**
## 13

### SEPTEMBER

| S | M | T | W | T | F | S |
|---|---|---|---|---|---|---|
|   |   | 1 | 2 | 3 | 4 | 5 |
| 6 | 7 | 8 | 9 | 10 | 11 | 12 |
| 13 | 14 | 15 | 16 | 17 | 18 | 19 |
| 20 | 21 | 22 | 23 | 24 | 25 | 26 |
| 27 | 28 | 29 | 30 |   |   |   |

### DIAMONDS OF BALI  90" x 90"
#### Janell Weinberger, Sun Prairie, WI

This quilt was paper pieced with over 1400 separate batik pieces, plus many hand-appliquéd diamonds. Janell colored the design on graph paper to decide on the arrangement of colors to create a medallion center blending into the pieced border. Machine quilted by Cindy Hasse of Cottage Grove, WI. A ribbon winner at the Prairie Heritage Show, Sun Prairie, WI and a Viewer's Choice winner at Piecemakers Quilt Show, Waunakee, WI.

Features Double Diamond Delight Pattern by Klaudeen Hansen.

# September

**14**

**15**

**16**

**17**

**18**        **Rosh Hashanah**

**19**

**20**

| SEPTEMBER | | | | | | |
|---|---|---|---|---|---|---|
| S | M | T | W | T | F | S |
|   |   | 1 | 2 | 3 | 4 | 5 |
| 6 | 7 | 8 | 9 | 10 | 11 | 12 |
| 13 | 14 | 15 | 16 | 17 | 18 | 19 |
| 20 | 21 | 22 | 23 | 24 | 25 | 26 |
| 27 | 28 | 29 | 30 |   |   |   |

### VILLAGE OF MY DREAMS    92" x 92"
#### Nancy Acker, Brodhead, WI

Hand appliqué is Nancy's favorite pastime, so when she saw this Kim McLean pattern with a ton of handwork, she knew it was her next quilt project. She selected many Kaffe Fassett print fabrics for the buildings, animals, and birds. The hexagons in the border were all hand-pieced. The quilt won the Best of Show at the Prairie Heritage Quilt Show, Sun Prairie, WI and was juried into Quilt Expo™, Madison, WI.

Features Village Pattern by Kim McLean, gloriouscolor.com.

# September

TUESDAY
22

WEDNESDAY
23

THURSDAY
24

FRIDAY
25

SATURDAY
26

SUNDAY
27

**Yom Kippur**

SEPTEMBER

| S | M | T | W | T | F | S |
|---|---|---|---|---|---|---|
|   |   | 1 | 2 | 3 | 4 | 5 |
| 6 | 7 | 8 | 9 | 10 | 11 | 12 |
| 13 | 14 | 15 | 16 | 17 | 18 | 19 |
| 20 | 21 | 22 | 23 | 24 | 25 | 26 |
| 27 | 28 | 29 | 30 |   |   |   |

### A WALK IN THE PARK  30" x 40"
**Pennee Clanton, Buffalo, SD**

For Pennee, working on the quilt design with her sister Kellee Mitchell was the most memorable part of this piece. It was inspired by an unsigned print Pennee saw in her hairdresser's salon. She did the appliqué and Kellee added the shadowing with fabric paints. Awarded Blue Ribbons at both the Black Hills Quilt Show, Rapid City and Prairie Points Show in Buffalo, SD, and a ribbon winner in the Fall Leaves Challenge at Quilt Expo™ in Madison, WI.

# September/October

MONDAY
## 28

TUESDAY
## 29

WEDNESDAY
## 30

THURSDAY
## 1

FRIDAY
## 2

SATURDAY
## 3

SUNDAY
## 4

OCTOBER

| S | M | T | W | T | F | S |
|---|---|---|---|---|---|---|
|   |   |   |   | 1 | 2 | 3 |
| 4 | 5 | 6 | 7 | 8 | 9 | 10 |
| 11 | 12 | 13 | 14 | 15 | 16 | 17 |
| 18 | 19 | 20 | 21 | 22 | 23 | 24 |
| 25 | 26 | 27 | 28 | 29 | 30 | 31 |

## AUTUMN BRAMBLE   44" x 44"
### Susan Nelson, Prior Lake, MN

This original design was created by Susan to fit a specific size and color scheme. An explosion of sharp points gives the illusion of a thorny, yet beautiful shrub. Constructed with paper piecing and curved piecing by machine. Susan used silk threads and a multitude of designs in the free-motion machine quilting. A ribbon winner in the Minnesota State Guild Show, St. Cloud, MN and juried into AQS Fall QuiltWeek®, Paducah, KY.

# October

MONDAY
## 5

TUESDAY
## 6

WEDNESDAY
## 7

THURSDAY
## 8

FRIDAY
## 9

SATURDAY
## 10

SUNDAY
## 11

OCTOBER

| S | M | T | W | T | F | S |
|---|---|---|---|---|---|---|
|   |   |   |   | 1 | 2 | 3 |
| 4 | 5 | 6 | 7 | 8 | 9 | 10 |
| 11 | 12 | 13 | 14 | 15 | 16 | 17 |
| 18 | 19 | 20 | 21 | 22 | 23 | 24 |
| 25 | 26 | 27 | 28 | 29 | 30 | 31 |

### AUTUMN, HARPER'S FERRY WV   52" x 48"
**Marlene Fenoglietto, Monroeville, PA**

Photography is another of Marlene's hobbies. The scene here is from a photo she took with intentions of depicting it in fabric. The most time-consuming part was the tiny piecing in the Log Cabin blocks for the sky and road. Choosing the fabric for buildings was fun, as Marlene planned to quilt each to simulate bricks or siding. Cotton fabrics were enhanced with some netting. Machine quilted by Marlene. Juried into AQS Spring QuiltWeek®, Paducah, KY.

# October

MONDAY
## 12
**Columbus Day**

TUESDAY
## 13

WEDNESDAY
## 14

THURSDAY
## 15

FRIDAY
## 16

SATURDAY
## 17

SUNDAY
## 18

### OCTOBER

| S | M | T | W | T | F | S |
|---|---|---|---|---|---|---|
|   |   |   |   | 1 | 2 | 3 |
| 4 | 5 | 6 | 7 | 8 | 9 | 10 |
| 11 | 12 | 13 | 14 | 15 | 16 | 17 |
| 18 | 19 | 20 | 21 | 22 | 23 | 24 |
| 25 | 26 | 27 | 28 | 29 | 30 | 31 |

## KALEIDOSCOPE COMPASSES   83" x 83"

### Kathleen Moorhead Johnson, Alexander, ND

Paula Nadelstern's fabric led Kathleen to design these five different compass blocks. Selecting additional prints and solids to complement each section was a fun part of the construction. The quilt is machine-pieced and machine-quilted, and has added ribbons to Kathleen's collection from Prairie Quilt Festival, Minot, ND, Metro Quilt Expo, Fargo, ND, and Minnesota State Show, St. Cloud, MN.

# October

## 19

## 20

WEDNESDAY
## 21

THURSDAY
## 22

FRIDAY
## 23

SATURDAY
## 24

SUNDAY
## 25

| | | | OCTOBER | | | |
|---|---|---|---|---|---|---|
| S | M | T | W | T | F | S |
| | | | | 1 | 2 | 3 |
| 4 | 5 | 6 | 7 | 8 | 9 | 10 |
| 11 | 12 | 13 | 14 | 15 | 16 | 17 |
| 18 | 19 | 20 | 21 | 22 | 23 | 24 |
| 25 | 26 | 27 | 28 | 29 | 30 | 31 |

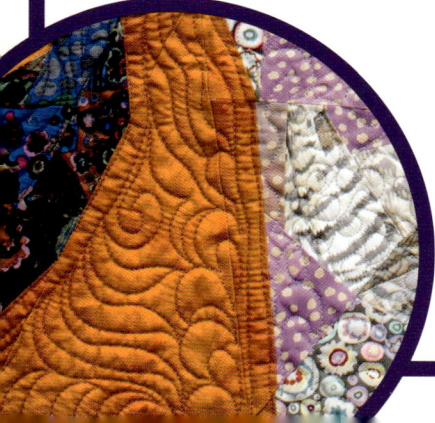

### CLEOPATRA  54" x 60"
#### Linda Crouch McCreadie, Gray, TN
Linda discovered that every paper piece unit was different in this Elephant Abstractions pattern by Violet Craft, making the project more time-consuming than she anticipated. She used Kaffe Fassett and Windham fabrics. To add expression to the eyes, Linda added some bits of white fabric. She machine quilted CLEOPATRA with free-motion designs. A ribbon winner at A Mountain Quiltfest, Pigeon Forge, TN.

Features Elephant Abstractions Pattern by Violet Craft, violetcraft.com.

# October/November

MONDAY
## 26

TUESDAY
## 27

WEDNESDAY
## 28

THURSDAY
## 29

FRIDAY
## 30

SATURDAY **Halloween**
## 31

SUNDAY **Daylight Saving Time ends**
## 1

| NOVEMBER | | | | | | |
|---|---|---|---|---|---|---|
| S | M | T | W | T | F | S |
| 1 | 2 | 3 | 4 | 5 | 6 | 7 |
| 8 | 9 | 10 | 11 | 12 | 13 | 14 |
| 15 | 16 | 17 | 18 | 19 | 20 | 21 |
| 22 | 23 | 24 | 25 | 26 | 27 | 28 |
| 29 | 30 | | | | | |

### GEORGIA ON MY MIND   35" x 35"
**Diane J. Evans, Schenectady, NY**

This quilt was inspired by musical mandalas and created for a group exhibit honoring the work of Georgia O'Keefe. The center is machine-appliquéd and enhanced with hand embroidery and handmade beads. Musical motifs were hand-inked by Diane before she added the machine quilting. The quilt was a multiple winner at Quilt Expo™, Madison, WI, Road to California, Ontario, CA, and Pacific International Festival, Santa Clara, CA. Juried into AQS QuiltWeek®, Syracuse, NY.

# November

MONDAY
## 2

TUESDAY
## 3
**Election Day**

WEDNESDAY
## 4

THURSDAY
## 5

FRIDAY
## 6

SATURDAY
## 7

SUNDAY
## 8

| | | NOVEMBER | | | | |
|---|---|---|---|---|---|---|
| S | M | T | W | T | F | S |
| 1 | 2 | 3 | 4 | 5 | 6 | 7 |
| 8 | 9 | 10 | 11 | 12 | 13 | 14 |
| 15 | 16 | 17 | 18 | 19 | 20 | 21 |
| 22 | 23 | 24 | 25 | 26 | 27 | 28 |
| 29 | 30 | | | | | |

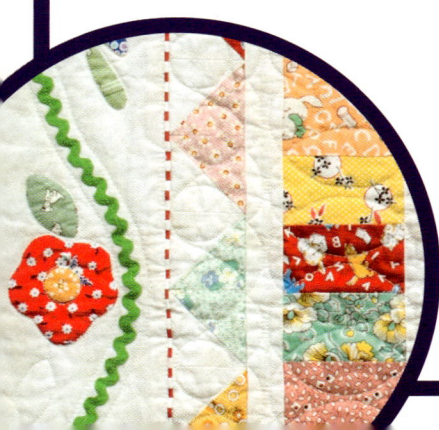

## DOT TO DOT    61" x 60"
### Cheryl Snellgrove, Autaugaville, AL

Inspired by four of Nancy Mahoney's patterns, this quilt includes turned-edge machine appliqué with invisible thread and machine piecing. The multitude of 30s fabrics reminded Cheryl of both of her grandmothers, as they were also quilters. Cheryl has made over 100 quilts and enjoyed adding this one's embellishments, which include red and white piping between borders and curved rickrack. Quilted by Cheryl on a stationary machine with some added embroidery stitches. Juried into the AQS QuiltWeek®, Fall Paducah and a winner at the National Fair, Montgomery, AL

Features Dot to Dot Pattern by Nancy Mahoney and Star Flower Baskets, A-Tisket A-Tasket, and Pinwheel Flowers from *Fast, Fusible Flower Quilts* by Nancy Mahoney © 2011 That Patchwork Place.

# November

MONDAY
## 9

TUESDAY
## 10

WEDNESDAY     **Veterans Day**
## 11

THURSDAY
## 12

FRIDAY
## 13

SATURDAY
## 14

SUNDAY
## 15

| NOVEMBER | | | | | | |
|---|---|---|---|---|---|---|
| S | M | T | W | T | F | S |
| 1 | 2 | 3 | 4 | 5 | 6 | 7 |
| 8 | 9 | 10 | 11 | 12 | 13 | 14 |
| 15 | 16 | 17 | 18 | 19 | 20 | 21 |
| 22 | 23 | 24 | 25 | 26 | 27 | 28 |
| 29 | 30 | | | | | |

*Happy Quilting*
*Judy*

## ENDLESS  57" x 58"

### Judy Lowery, Franklin, NC

After paper piecing several patterns, Judy decided to try this circular Jacqueline de Jonge design. She found it challenging to learn a new method to handle the 1364 pieces! Her color idea changed as she worked, and she replaced many fabrics from the purchased kit with favorite pieces from her own stash. Machine quilted by Kathy Stuart in tiny pebbles and intricate feathers. A ribbon winner at both Sauder Village Quilt Show, Archbold, OH and Kaleidoscope of Quilts, Sylvania, OH.

Features Endless Pattern by Jacqueline de Jonge, becolourful.com.

# November

MONDAY
## 16

TUESDAY
## 17

WEDNESDAY
## 18

THURSDAY
## 19

FRIDAY
## 20

SATURDAY
## 21

SUNDAY
## 22

### NOVEMBER

| S | M | T | W | T | F | S |
|---|---|---|---|---|---|---|
| 1 | 2 | 3 | 4 | 5 | 6 | 7 |
| 8 | 9 | 10 | 11 | 12 | 13 | 14 |
| 15 | 16 | 17 | 18 | 19 | 20 | 21 |
| 22 | 23 | 24 | 25 | 26 | 27 | 28 |
| 29 | 30 | | | | | |

### ARROWHEADS   71" x 71"

**Stephanie Parks, Minneapolis, MN**

Stephanie desiged traditional New York Beauty blocks in EQ7, then machine pieced them with foundation papers. Her collection of fabrics included shot cottons by Kaffe Fassett, Civil War reproductions, and several plaids and checks. She arranged the blocks in a new setting with pieced sashing and cornerposts. Machine quilted by Just Sew Studio, St. Louis Park, MN with a computerized design called "Pick-up Sticks".

# November

MONDAY
## 23

TUESDAY
## 24

WEDNESDAY
## 25

THURSDAY
## 26
**Thanksgiving Day**

FRIDAY
## 27

SATURDAY
## 28

SUNDAY
## 29

| NOVEMBER | | | | | | |
|---|---|---|---|---|---|---|
| S | M | T | W | T | F | S |
| 1 | 2 | 3 | 4 | 5 | 6 | 7 |
| 8 | 9 | 10 | 11 | 12 | 13 | 14 |
| 15 | 16 | 17 | 18 | 19 | 20 | 21 |
| 22 | 23 | 24 | 25 | 26 | 27 | 28 |
| 29 | 30 | | | | | |

### BECAUSE I CAN  105" x 105"
### Angela Wirth, Ellsworth, IA

Making this pattern by Jackie Robinson was the first time Angela used strip piecing, for the diamonds. The thirteen purple and orange fabrics were picked in one trip to one shop! Angela did her own machine quilting with wool batting and put different designs in each of the eight blocks surrounding the center. Straight lines accented with feathers and pebbles completed the quilting. The quilt was juried into Quilt Festival, Shipshewana, IN.

Features Lone Star Pizzazz Pattern by Jackie Robinson, animasquilts.com.

# November/December

MONDAY
## 30

TUESDAY
## 1

WEDNESDAY
## 2

THURSDAY
## 3

FRIDAY
## 4

SATURDAY
## 5

SUNDAY
## 6

### DECEMBER

| S | M | T | W | T | F | S |
|---|---|---|---|---|---|---|
|   |   | 1 | 2 | 3 | 4 | 5 |
| 6 | 7 | 8 | 9 | 10 | 11 | 12 |
| 13 | 14 | 15 | 16 | 17 | 18 | 19 |
| 20 | 21 | 22 | 23 | 24 | 25 | 26 |
| 27 | 28 | 29 | 30 | 31 |   |   |

## QUINTET OF KLIMT   49" x 59"
### Marsha Walper, Tallahassee, FL

Inspired by a class taught by Linda Sullivan, designer of the "curly trees". Marsha hand appliquéd the trees and curls, and the traditional blocks are machine-pieced. Both hand quilting and machine quilting were done by Marsha. A first place winner at Capital City Quilt Show, Tallahassee, FL. Juried into AQS QuiltWeek®, Spring Paducah, KY and at QuiltFest Jax, Jacksonville, FL.

*Features Curly Trees Pattern from workshop by Linda O'Sullivan.*

# December

**Hanukkah begins**

### DECEMBER

| S | M | T | W | T | F | S |
|---|---|---|---|---|---|---|
|   |   | 1 | 2 | 3 | 4 | 5 |
| 6 | 7 | 8 | 9 | 10 | 11 | 12 |
| 13 | 14 | 15 | 16 | 17 | 18 | 19 |
| 20 | 21 | 22 | 23 | 24 | 25 | 26 |
| 27 | 28 | 29 | 30 | 31 |   |   |

### RINGS, CIRCLES & FANS   90" x 92"
#### Susan Haslett-Scholfield, Canton, MI

Kaffe Fassett prints were fun for Susan to machine piece into this design by Lessa Siefele. The cutting process was a bit time consuming, as it contains 3500+ pieces! Susan did her own quilting on her APQS George stationary machine; some free motion, some stencil work, and Baptist Fans on the borders. A blue ribbon winner at Sauder Village Quilt Show, Archbold, OH, and juried into Quilt Festival, Shipshewana, IN and AQS Fall QuiltWeek®, Fall Paducah, KY and Virginia Beach, VA.

*Features Ring Cycles Quilt Pattern by Lessa Siegele.*

# December

**MONDAY**
## 14

**TUESDAY**
## 15

**WEDNESDAY**
## 16

**THURSDAY**
## 17

**FRIDAY**
## 18
**Hanukkah (last day)**

**SATURDAY**
## 19

**SUNDAY**
## 20

DECEMBER

| S | M | T | W | T | F | S |
|---|---|---|---|---|---|---|
|   |   | 1 | 2 | 3 | 4 | 5 |
| 6 | 7 | 8 | 9 | 10 | 11 | 12 |
| 13 | 14 | 15 | 16 | 17 | 18 | 19 |
| 20 | 21 | 22 | 23 | 24 | 25 | 26 |
| 27 | 28 | 29 | 30 | 31 |   |   |

### MOSAIC MEDLEY AT MIDNIGHT  80" x 80"
**Nancy Kay Smith, Belleview, FL**

A visit to the Seminole Indian Village and watching the ladies sewing on their hand crank machines led Nancy Kay to try several different Seminole-style designs. She started with graph paper and colored pencils, then moved on to batik fabrics. Piping is featured on each side of the strips. Machine quilted by Nancy Kay on her Bernina 440. A ribbon winner at QuiltFest Jax, Jacksonville, FL, World Quilt Show, Orlando, FL, and Quilt Odyssey, Hershey, PA and juried into AQS QuiltWeek®, Spring Paducah, KY and Daytona, FL.

# December

**21**

**22**

**23**

**24**

**25**          **Christmas Day**

**26**

**27**

### DECEMBER

| S | M | T | W | T | F | S |
|---|---|---|---|---|---|---|
|   |   | 1 | 2 | 3 | 4 | 5 |
| 6 | 7 | 8 | 9 | 10 | 11 | 12 |
| 13 | 14 | 15 | 16 | 17 | 18 | 19 |
| 20 | 21 | 22 | 23 | 24 | 25 | 26 |
| 27 | 28 | 29 | 30 | 31 |   |   |

*Happy stitching!* *Cassandra d Beaver*

## COMPLEMENTARY COMPOSITION  63" x 69"
### Cassandra Ireland Beaver, Urbana, OH

A challenge issued by the Modern Quilt Guild was the inspiration for Cassandra to use these vibrant colors in creating an improvisational pieced composition. The quilt was pieced on her Bernina 1008, with some slivers of fabric a mere ⅛" wide. Scale and proportion are further emphasized with linear quilting and a range of angles to add visual energy to the quilt. Juried into AQS Spring QuiltWeek® Paducah, KY.

# December/January

## 28

## 29

## 30

## 31

## 1
**New Year's Day**

## 2

## 3

| JANUARY | | | | | | |
|---|---|---|---|---|---|---|
| S | M | T | W | T | F | S |
|   |   |   |   |   | 1 | 2 |
| 3 | 4 | 5 | 6 | 7 | 8 | 9 |
| 10 | 11 | 12 | 13 | 14 | 15 | 16 |
| 17 | 18 | 19 | 20 | 21 | 22 | 23 |
| 24 | 25 | 26 | 27 | 28 | 29 | 30 |
| 31 |   |   |   |   |   |   |

# Projects

Project Name_____

Materials Needed:

_____   _____   _____

_____   _____   _____

_____   _____   _____

Notes:

_____

_____

_____

_____

Project Name_____

Materials Needed:

_____   _____   _____

_____   _____   _____

_____   _____   _____

Notes:

_____

_____

_____

_____

# Projects

Project Name_____

Materials Needed:

_____   _____   _____

_____   _____   _____

_____   _____   _____

Notes:

_____

_____

_____

_____

Project Name_____

Materials Needed:

_____   _____   _____

_____   _____   _____

_____   _____   _____

Notes:

_____

_____

_____

_____

# Projects

Project Name_____

Materials Needed:

_____    _____    _____

_____    _____    _____

_____    _____    _____

Notes:

_____

_____

_____

_____

Project Name_____

Materials Needed:

_____    _____    _____

_____    _____    _____

_____    _____    _____

Notes:

_____

_____

_____

_____

# Projects

Project Name _____

Materials Needed:

_____     _____     _____

_____     _____     _____

_____     _____     _____

Notes:

_____

_____

_____

_____

_____

Project Name _____

Materials Needed:

_____     _____     _____

_____     _____     _____

_____     _____     _____

Notes:

_____

_____

_____

_____

# UFO's

Project Name_____

Materials Needed:

_____     _____     _____

_____     _____     _____

Notes:

_____

Project Name_____

Materials Needed:

_____     _____     _____

Notes:

_____

_____

Project Name_____

Materials Needed:

_____     _____     _____

Notes:

_____

_____

# UFO's

Project Name_____

Materials Needed:

_____    _____    _____

_____    _____    _____

Notes:

_____


Project Name_____

Materials Needed:

_____    _____    _____

Notes:

_____

_____


Project Name_____

Materials Needed:

_____    _____    _____

Notes:

_____

_____

# UFO's

Project Name_____

Materials Needed:

_____ _____ _____

_____ _____ _____

Notes:

_____

Project Name_____

Materials Needed:

_____ _____ _____

Notes:

_____

_____

Project Name_____

Materials Needed:

_____ _____ _____

Notes:

_____

_____

# UFO's

Project Name_____

Materials Needed:

_____    _____    _____

_____    _____    _____

Notes:

_____

Project Name_____

Materials Needed:

_____    _____    _____

Notes:

_____

_____

Project Name_____

Materials Needed:

_____    _____    _____

Notes:

_____

_____

# Machine Maintenance

Machine Name _____

Date: _____      Reason: _____

Repair Shop _____      Phone: _____      Cost _____

Machine Name _____

Date: _____      Reason: _____

Repair Shop _____      Phone: _____      Cost _____

Machine Name _____

Date: _____      Reason: _____

Repair Shop _____      Phone: _____      Cost _____

Machine Name _____

Date: _____      Reason: _____

Repair Shop _____      Phone: _____      Cost _____

Mark when you clean your machine:

|   | J | F | M | A | M | J | J | A | S | O | N | D |
|---|---|---|---|---|---|---|---|---|---|---|---|---|
| 1 |   |   |   |   |   |   |   |   |   |   |   |   |
| 2 |   |   |   |   |   |   |   |   |   |   |   |   |
| 3 |   |   |   |   |   |   |   |   |   |   |   |   |
| 4 |   |   |   |   |   |   |   |   |   |   |   |   |

# Goals for Next Year

_____

_____

_____

_____

_____

_____

_____

_____

_____

_____

_____

_____

_____

_____

_____

_____

# Addresses & Birthdays

Name_____     Phone_____

Email_____Birthday_____

Address_____

_____


Name_____     Phone_____

Email_____Birthday_____

Address_____

_____


Name_____     Phone_____

Email_____Birthday_____

Address_____

_____


Name_____     Phone_____

Email_____Birthday_____

Address_____

_____


Name_____     Phone_____

Email_____Birthday_____

Address_____

_____

# Addresses & Birthdays

Name _____ Phone _____

Email _____ Birthday _____

Address _____

_____

Name _____ Phone _____

Email _____ Birthday _____

Address _____

_____

Name _____ Phone _____

Email _____ Birthday _____

Address _____

_____

Name _____ Phone _____

Email _____ Birthday _____

Address _____

_____

Name _____ Phone _____

Email _____ Birthday _____

Address _____

_____

# Addresses & Birthdays

Name _____ Phone _____

Email _____ Birthday _____

Address _____

_____


Name _____ Phone _____

Email _____ Birthday _____

Address _____

_____


Name _____ Phone _____

Email _____ Birthday _____

Address _____

_____


Name _____ Phone _____

Email _____ Birthday _____

Address _____

_____


Name _____ Phone _____

Email _____ Birthday _____

Address _____

_____

# Addresses & Birthdays

Name_____     Phone _____

Email _____     Birthday _____

Address_____

_____


Name_____     Phone _____

Email _____     Birthday _____

Address_____

_____


Name_____     Phone _____

Email _____     Birthday _____

Address_____

_____


Name_____     Phone _____

Email _____     Birthday _____

Address_____

_____


Name_____     Phone _____

Email _____     Birthday _____

Address_____

_____

# Addresses & Birthdays

Name _____  Phone _____

Email _____ Birthday _____

Address _____

_____


Name _____  Phone _____

Email _____ Birthday _____

Address _____

_____


Name _____  Phone _____

Email _____ Birthday _____

Address _____

_____


Name _____  Phone _____

Email _____ Birthday _____

Address _____

_____


Name _____  Phone _____

Email _____ Birthday _____

Address _____

_____

# Addresses & Birthdays

Name _____ Phone _____

Email _____ Birthday _____

Address _____

_____


Name _____ Phone _____

Email _____ Birthday _____

Address _____

_____


Name _____ Phone _____

Email _____ Birthday _____

Address _____

_____


Name _____ Phone _____

Email _____ Birthday _____

Address _____

_____


Name _____ Phone _____

Email _____ Birthday _____

Address _____

_____

# Notes

# 2020 QUILT**ART** Engagement Calendar
## A year full of fabulous quilts!

Klaudeen Hansen

*Klaudeen Hansen presents QuiltArt 2020. This collection of 54 visually stunning and award-winning quilts was selected from a field of 5380. Klaudeen combines the best in workmanship, fabric selection, original design, and interpretation of classic patterns in this yearlong planner.*

*Each week of the year brings you a new quilt with a turn of the page. Use the week-at-a-glance pages to keep up with appointments, things to do, and places to go.*

*Take advantage of Klaudeen's travels to teach and lecture at quilt shows and conferences as you move through the year. QuiltArt allows you to stay on track while enjoying quilts that will amaze and inspire.*

*Copy Editor: Hannah Alton*
*Graphic Designer: Lynda Smith*

---

*Additional copies of this calendar may be obtained from your favorite bookseller, sewing center, or craft shop, or from:*

**American Quilter's Society**
**PO Box 3290**
**Paducah, KY 42002-3290**
**1-800-626-5420 • fax (270) 898-1173**
**www.AmericanQuilter.com**

*$15.95 per copy*

*The publisher has made every effort to ensure the accuracy of information in this calendar but cannot assume liability for any errors.*

# 2020

## JANUARY
| S | M | T | W | T | F | S |
|---|---|---|---|---|---|---|
|   |   |   | 1 | 2 | 3 | 4 |
| 5 | 6 | 7 | 8 | 9 | 10 | 11 |
| 12 | 13 | 14 | 15 | 16 | 17 | 18 |
| 19 | 20 | 21 | 22 | 23 | 24 | 25 |
| 26 | 27 | 28 | 29 | 30 | 31 |   |

## FEBRUARY
| S | M | T | W | T | F | S |
|---|---|---|---|---|---|---|
|   |   |   |   |   |   | 1 |
| 2 | 3 | 4 | 5 | 6 | 7 | 8 |
| 9 | 10 | 11 | 12 | 13 | 14 | 15 |
| 16 | 17 | 18 | 19 | 20 | 21 | 22 |
| 23 | 24 | 25 | 26 | 27 | 28 | 29 |

## MARCH
| S | M | T | W | T | F | S |
|---|---|---|---|---|---|---|
| 1 | 2 | 3 | 4 | 5 | 6 | 7 |
| 8 | 9 | 10 | 11 | 12 | 13 | 14 |
| 15 | 16 | 17 | 18 | 19 | 20 | 21 |
| 22 | 23 | 24 | 25 | 26 | 27 | 28 |
| 29 | 30 | 31 |   |   |   |   |

## APRIL
| S | M | T | W | T | F | S |
|---|---|---|---|---|---|---|
|   |   |   | 1 | 2 | 3 | 4 |
| 5 | 6 | 7 | 8 | 9 | 10 | 11 |
| 12 | 13 | 14 | 15 | 16 | 17 | 18 |
| 19 | 20 | 21 | 22 | 23 | 24 | 25 |
| 26 | 27 | 28 | 29 | 30 |   |   |

## MAY
| S | M | T | W | T | F | S |
|---|---|---|---|---|---|---|
|   |   |   |   |   | 1 | 2 |
| 3 | 4 | 5 | 6 | 7 | 8 | 9 |
| 10 | 11 | 12 | 13 | 14 | 15 | 16 |
| 17 | 18 | 19 | 20 | 21 | 22 | 23 |
| 24 | 25 | 26 | 27 | 28 | 29 | 30 |
| 31 |   |   |   |   |   |   |

## JUNE
| S | M | T | W | T | F | S |
|---|---|---|---|---|---|---|
|   | 1 | 2 | 3 | 4 | 5 | 6 |
| 7 | 8 | 9 | 10 | 11 | 12 | 13 |
| 14 | 15 | 16 | 17 | 18 | 19 | 20 |
| 21 | 22 | 23 | 24 | 25 | 26 | 27 |
| 28 | 29 | 30 |   |   |   |   |

## JULY
| S | M | T | W | T | F | S |
|---|---|---|---|---|---|---|
|   |   |   | 1 | 2 | 3 | 4 |
| 5 | 6 | 7 | 8 | 9 | 10 | 11 |
| 12 | 13 | 14 | 15 | 16 | 17 | 18 |
| 19 | 20 | 21 | 22 | 23 | 24 | 25 |
| 26 | 27 | 28 | 29 | 30 | 31 |   |

## AUGUST
| S | M | T | W | T | F | S |
|---|---|---|---|---|---|---|
|   |   |   |   |   |   | 1 |
| 2 | 3 | 4 | 5 | 6 | 7 | 8 |
| 9 | 10 | 11 | 12 | 13 | 14 | 15 |
| 16 | 17 | 18 | 19 | 20 | 21 | 22 |
| 23 | 24 | 25 | 26 | 27 | 28 | 29 |
| 30 | 31 |   |   |   |   |   |

## SEPTEMBER
| S | M | T | W | T | F | S |
|---|---|---|---|---|---|---|
|   |   | 1 | 2 | 3 | 4 | 5 |
| 6 | 7 | 8 | 9 | 10 | 11 | 12 |
| 13 | 14 | 15 | 16 | 17 | 18 | 19 |
| 20 | 21 | 22 | 23 | 24 | 25 | 26 |
| 27 | 28 | 29 | 30 |   |   |   |

## OCTOBER
| S | M | T | W | T | F | S |
|---|---|---|---|---|---|---|
|   |   |   |   | 1 | 2 | 3 |
| 4 | 5 | 6 | 7 | 8 | 9 | 10 |
| 11 | 12 | 13 | 14 | 15 | 16 | 17 |
| 18 | 19 | 20 | 21 | 22 | 23 | 24 |
| 25 | 26 | 27 | 28 | 29 | 30 | 31 |

## NOVEMBER
| S | M | T | W | T | F | S |
|---|---|---|---|---|---|---|
| 1 | 2 | 3 | 4 | 5 | 6 | 7 |
| 8 | 9 | 10 | 11 | 12 | 13 | 14 |
| 15 | 16 | 17 | 18 | 19 | 20 | 21 |
| 22 | 23 | 24 | 25 | 26 | 27 | 28 |
| 29 | 30 |   |   |   |   |   |

## DECEMBER
| S | M | T | W | T | F | S |
|---|---|---|---|---|---|---|
|   |   | 1 | 2 | 3 | 4 | 5 |
| 6 | 7 | 8 | 9 | 10 | 11 | 12 |
| 13 | 14 | 15 | 16 | 17 | 18 | 19 |
| 20 | 21 | 22 | 23 | 24 | 25 | 26 |
| 27 | 28 | 29 | 30 | 31 |   |   |

# 2021

## JANUARY
| S | M | T | W | T | F | S |
|---|---|---|---|---|---|---|
|   |   |   |   |   | 1 | 2 |
| 3 | 4 | 5 | 6 | 7 | 8 | 9 |
| 10 | 11 | 12 | 13 | 14 | 15 | 16 |
| 17 | 18 | 19 | 20 | 21 | 22 | 23 |
| 24 | 25 | 26 | 27 | 28 | 29 | 30 |
| 31 |   |   |   |   |   |   |

## FEBRUARY
| S | M | T | W | T | F | S |
|---|---|---|---|---|---|---|
|   | 1 | 2 | 3 | 4 | 5 | 6 |
| 7 | 8 | 9 | 10 | 11 | 12 | 13 |
| 14 | 15 | 16 | 17 | 18 | 19 | 20 |
| 21 | 22 | 23 | 24 | 25 | 26 | 27 |
| 28 |   |   |   |   |   |   |

## MARCH
| S | M | T | W | T | F | S |
|---|---|---|---|---|---|---|
|   | 1 | 2 | 3 | 4 | 5 | 6 |
| 7 | 8 | 9 | 10 | 11 | 12 | 13 |
| 14 | 15 | 16 | 17 | 18 | 19 | 20 |
| 21 | 22 | 23 | 24 | 25 | 26 | 27 |
| 28 | 29 | 30 | 31 |   |   |   |

## APRIL
| S | M | T | W | T | F | S |
|---|---|---|---|---|---|---|
|   |   |   |   | 1 | 2 | 3 |
| 4 | 5 | 6 | 7 | 8 | 9 | 10 |
| 11 | 12 | 13 | 14 | 15 | 16 | 17 |
| 18 | 19 | 20 | 21 | 22 | 23 | 24 |
| 25 | 26 | 27 | 28 | 29 | 30 |   |

## MAY
| S | M | T | W | T | F | S |
|---|---|---|---|---|---|---|
|   |   |   |   |   |   | 1 |
| 2 | 3 | 4 | 5 | 6 | 7 | 8 |
| 9 | 10 | 11 | 12 | 13 | 14 | 15 |
| 16 | 17 | 18 | 19 | 20 | 21 | 22 |
| 23 | 24 | 25 | 26 | 27 | 28 | 29 |
| 30 | 31 |   |   |   |   |   |

## JUNE
| S | M | T | W | T | F | S |
|---|---|---|---|---|---|---|
|   |   | 1 | 2 | 3 | 4 | 5 |
| 6 | 7 | 8 | 9 | 10 | 11 | 12 |
| 13 | 14 | 15 | 16 | 17 | 18 | 19 |
| 20 | 21 | 22 | 23 | 24 | 25 | 26 |
| 27 | 28 | 29 | 30 |   |   |   |

## JULY
| S | M | T | W | T | F | S |
|---|---|---|---|---|---|---|
|   |   |   |   | 1 | 2 | 3 |
| 4 | 5 | 6 | 7 | 8 | 9 | 10 |
| 11 | 12 | 13 | 14 | 15 | 16 | 17 |
| 18 | 19 | 20 | 21 | 22 | 23 | 24 |
| 25 | 26 | 27 | 28 | 29 | 30 | 31 |

## AUGUST
| S | M | T | W | T | F | S |
|---|---|---|---|---|---|---|
| 1 | 2 | 3 | 4 | 5 | 6 | 7 |
| 8 | 9 | 10 | 11 | 12 | 13 | 14 |
| 15 | 16 | 17 | 18 | 19 | 20 | 21 |
| 22 | 23 | 24 | 25 | 26 | 27 | 28 |
| 29 | 30 | 31 |   |   |   |   |

## SEPTEMBER
| S | M | T | W | T | F | S |
|---|---|---|---|---|---|---|
|   |   |   | 1 | 2 | 3 | 4 |
| 5 | 6 | 7 | 8 | 9 | 10 | 11 |
| 12 | 13 | 14 | 15 | 16 | 17 | 18 |
| 19 | 20 | 21 | 22 | 23 | 24 | 25 |
| 26 | 27 | 28 | 29 | 30 |   |   |

## OCTOBER
| S | M | T | W | T | F | S |
|---|---|---|---|---|---|---|
|   |   |   |   |   | 1 | 2 |
| 3 | 4 | 5 | 6 | 7 | 8 | 9 |
| 10 | 11 | 12 | 13 | 14 | 15 | 16 |
| 17 | 18 | 19 | 20 | 21 | 22 | 23 |
| 24 | 25 | 26 | 27 | 28 | 29 | 30 |
| 31 |   |   |   |   |   |   |

## NOVEMBER
| S | M | T | W | T | F | S |
|---|---|---|---|---|---|---|
|   | 1 | 2 | 3 | 4 | 5 | 6 |
| 7 | 8 | 9 | 10 | 11 | 12 | 13 |
| 14 | 15 | 16 | 17 | 18 | 19 | 20 |
| 21 | 22 | 23 | 24 | 25 | 26 | 27 |
| 28 | 29 | 30 |   |   |   |   |

## DECEMBER
| S | M | T | W | T | F | S |
|---|---|---|---|---|---|---|
|   |   |   | 1 | 2 | 3 | 4 |
| 5 | 6 | 7 | 8 | 9 | 10 | 11 |
| 12 | 13 | 14 | 15 | 16 | 17 | 18 |
| 19 | 20 | 21 | 22 | 23 | 24 | 25 |
| 26 | 27 | 28 | 29 | 30 | 31 |   |